It was a great day to go out and play.

Ned had his hat on his head.

He put on one boot and then the other.

When he went out, Ned saw many
of his friends from school.
And every one of them had a new sled!
Ned didn't have a new sled,
so he went back in the house.

Ned started to take off his boots.

"Why are you back in?" asked his father.

"My sled is old, and all of my friends
have new sleds," said Ned.

"Come with me," said his father.

"I have the right thing for you."

Ned and his father went to the back of the house.

Ned's father took out a sled.

It was old and it was big.

It was made out of wood.

"This was my sled when I was little,"
said Ned's father.
"Before that it was my father's sled.
Now it will be your new old sled!"

At first Ned didn't like the old sled.

He didn't see how it could look new.

He thought, "It's too big and too old.

It looks funny."

But then Ned's father went to work.
He made the sled look good.

Ned and his father took the sled out.

Ned's friends came to look at it.

They said, "It's too big and too old.

It looks funny."

Then Ned's father said,
"This sled IS old, but it works.
Would you like to take
a turn with us?"

Ned's friends looked at each other.

Then they all said, "We'll try it."

"Get on! Get set!" said Ned's father.

"HERE WE GO!"

They started down.

ZOOM! The sled was fast!

It flew down, but no one was afraid.

It was fun!

Ned and his friends played
with the sled all day.
It was old and it was big.
But it was fast, and it was fun.

"It's a good thing you didn't throw this sled out,"
Ned said to his father.

"I had a great time with my new old sled!"